C000177308

Discov
Your
Destination

Cormac Noonan

Copyright © 2019 Cormac Noonan

All rights reserved.

ISBN: 9781707023370

DEDICATION

This book is dedicated to my parents, Michael and Caitriona. Firstly for supporting me through my four years in college and secondly for not disowning me when I decided to throw it all away in search of something else. Without your continued belief in me (and financial support), I'm not sure where I'd be.

CONTENTS

INTRODUCTION

Why I wrote this book - My Career Story

I live a very happy, carefree and fulfilling life. I am both happy with my current position and excited about where I am going in the future. I have created a life that enables me to do the work that I am passionate about. I currently work as a writer as well as a life and career coach.

Not only do I have a passion for what I do, but the work I do helps improve other people's lives while also funding my ability to enjoy my own. On top of this, my current work also helps keep me moving towards my overarching long-term goal working towards transforming the educational system in Ireland.

But life wasn't always like this for me. I didn't always live a carefree life, working on things I'm passionate about and traveling the world. Back in 2014, I had just finished my degree and I was deciding which direction to take after university. I had followed the path excellently so far. At least the path society told me to follow. I made it into Trinity College Dublin, which was the most recognized university in Ireland at the time. This was praised as a good achievement as not many went there from my secondary school. Part of the reason for this may have been because people from Navan (my home town in Ireland) looked at it as a posh school and didn't want to go there. But I didn't care about whether it was upmarket or not. It was still the most recognized university in Ireland and I firmly believed, based on what I had been told up until that point, that going there would give me the best possible opportunity for my future career.

I looked on as my friends headed off to other universities in Dublin while I took the lonely road to the big, posh school to join the D4s (a name given to people living in a well-off area of Dublin). Growing up playing Gaelic Football in County Meath, I was bred to scorn people from Dublin and to me, the D4s were the worst of a bad bunch. And despite the deterrent of having no friends there along with my perceived struggle to co-inhabit a space with the annoying D4s (some of them turned out to be ok in the end), I still decided to go to Trinity. That's how determined I was to succeed in my career.

Even since my secondary school days, I've had a drive to succeed in my career. Unlike many of my friends, my parents never had to push me to study for the Leaving Cert. In fact, it was quite the opposite. My mother would often come into my study area and plead with me "Cor have you not done enough work for the evening? Come out here and relax". "Just one more hour Mam" I'd tell her, "then I'll come out and watch TV?".

I also asked my mother to bring me to a good career counsellor to help steer me towards the right degree. I didn't want to waste years studying something that wasn't my true calling. I wanted to study something that gave me the best opportunity to do all the things I wanted to do in my future. The counsellor was good and she made me aware of a course called Management Science and Information Systems Studies. It was relatively unknown at the time but it covered a wide range of areas from Maths to Business to Statistics to IT. I was very Maths and Business focused and I was aware that the future was in IT so the course seemed the perfect fit. It would open up opportunities in many areas for me and give me a solid IT background.

Throughout my college years I actively sought out mentors. During a summer internship in my third year, I was assigned a mentor by the company I was working for. I would arrive at each meeting with a page full of questions, curious about what it was I should be looking for in a career. Where did family, friends, and hobbies such as football rank alongside work in the list of priorities? What were the trends of the future? Where was the money at? What skills did I need to work on to get there? What extra courses or things could I study now to get ahead of the rest?

Upon graduating I carved out my own role in a startup company with whom I had worked with for my Final Year Project. It was a Research and Analytics based role and it was a hot area at the time. I spent six months there before starting my graduate role in Accenture.

Apparently, this was one of the best and highest-paid graduate roles you could land. I didn't know too much about all of the big companies before moving up to Dublin but I had listened to friends who all seemed to know the ins and outs. Many of them came from private schools and seemed to have a predetermined career path in their heads. Coming from "the country" in County Meath, I was never made aware of any of these career paths but I had the drive to go for the best jobs and I listened to the advice of my peers. After spending almost three years working in Accenture, I realized I had made a big mistake. I decided that in order to be happy, I had to quit and pursue something I was passionate about.

Looking back, I realize that I had been sucked into the mentality of the crowd. I had been fooled into thinking I was searching for my own true path. Instead, I was listening to the advice of others on what they thought were the best careers.

Why you should read this book

This book will cover everything you need to know about choosing the right career path. Notice I used the word right instead of best. I'm here to help you discover the right path for you specifically. There are many people out there boasting that they have the best careers but just because they love it doesn't mean you will.

I don't want you to waste years of your life chasing other people's career goals. Instead, I want to help you discover your own destination. This book will cut through all of the current noise and confusion about careers that currently surrounds most of you. The book will help you discover what your mission is, what your core values are and how you can incorporate these into the type of work you choose to do. This book will then give you the tools necessary to create a crystal-clear vision for the career and life you want to have.

I must stress, however, that simply reading the book will not manifest your dream career. It can serve as an excellent guide but only if you put in the work. You must choose to be honest with yourself in the exercises and dig deep to find your true mission and your true values.

Your career is going to have a large impact on determining who you become, the people with whom you spend most of your time and the impact you have on the world. We spend over one-third of our lives at work so if you want to look back on your life without regret, then I suggest you make sure it is a career of your choosing.

This book is not designed to give you advice on what career to pursue. I don't know you personally so I can't advise you on it. This book is designed to get you to ask yourself the right questions rather than to try and give you the answers.

We've all grown up with unique experiences. We each have distinct fond memories of our pasts and we each have gone through different struggles. It follows that there is no one answer to what drives each of us. However, there are questions that can help us discover these deep motivations. I hope to help you articulate your unique drive so that you can create a vision for how you can positively channel it into the work that you do.

CHAPTER 1:
REALIZE YOUR MAP IS WRONG

"What we know is a drop, what we don't know is an ocean" - Isaac Newton

One of the first presuppositions of Neuro-Linguistic Programming is to recognize that your beliefs about the world are true only from your perspective. Throughout your past life experiences, you have only been able to see a portion of the map. Nobody on earth has the entire map, showing how everything fits together, including all the bumps and undulations. The reason for almost every argument we have with someone is because our map differs from their map. Each person has experienced life differently thus we all see the world differently. Even if you had a twin with whom you grew up with and shared the same experiences with, you both would have created different meanings for each experience and thus you both would have different maps of how the world works.

Why is This Important?

At times we can all be quite stubborn in our views of the world. Oftentimes we find that we prefer to win arguments to back up our beliefs rather than to get to the truth. By understanding that our maps are flawed, as well as everyone else's, we can open ourselves up to viewing other people's maps with curiosity instead of judgment. This will improve our relationships and help to prevent misunderstandings which lead to arguments.

It is also important to realize that our maps have been strongly influenced by the place in which we grew up and by the people with whom we have been surrounded by since we were young. Creating our maps based on the people around us often leads us to believe that our potential is limited to that of those within our community. If we are driven, we might look at the "successful" members of our community and strive towards emulating them.

The most influential and rich man in your neighbourhood may be a doctor and you, therefore, develop the belief that to be wealthy and well-respected you should pursue the same path. It is the beliefs we develop at a young age that are what often leads us towards our future careers. By being trapped in the mindset of the community we never really question our beliefs. Others within the same community only reinforce our beliefs that the path we are on is the right one. This is what I believe often leads many people towards having mid-life crises in their 40s and 50s. They finally come to the realization that they didn't actually choose their own path but instead followed the path laid out for them by those around them.

Today We Can See More of The Map

Nowadays, most of us are much more disconnected from our local communities than we would have been only 20 years ago. While I believe strongly in the importance of community, maybe one potential benefit of the disconnect is that we are no longer blinded by the common beliefs of the community members.

The internet has allowed us to look beyond our community for new role models and different ways of living and working. Through social media, we are beginning to see a bit more of the map and what the actual terrain looks like. This helps us realize that there are more options out there for our future careers. We are no longer destined to take over the family farm and it is rare that we come under pressure to become the local doctor or parish priest.

The Opportunities are Limitless

It is important that we realize how we are a product of the people around us and that our beliefs about what a good career is have been shaped by the area in which we grew up. This encourages us to stop focusing on our narrow, limited section of the map. It enables us to take a step back and look at the map through a wider lens.

The truth is, there are unlimited possibilities out there for you to decide what you want to do with your life and career. I say both life and career as I believe they go hand-in-hand. I believe your career should complement your life rather than be separate from it. Working in a career that doesn't align with your core values and what you believe is right will eventually eat away at your integrity and self-worth.

Don't Settle For Something You Don't Believe In

If honesty is one of your core values and you work for a company that promotes health-damaging products to unsuspecting customers, what will happen to your integrity and self-worth after contributing to thousands of illnesses throughout your years working for the company?

You might say you are just doing it for the money but you must ask yourself if that amount of money is enough compensation for living in constant conflict with your beliefs. Maybe it is worth it. Maybe the money you make from the job that you don't like gives you the free time and resources to do the things you do like. If so, that's great. But you must ask yourself what you are sacrificing while you are in work. For example, being a lawyer is the best-paid job in the USA but lawyers are 3.6 times more likely to be depressed.[1]

A 2017 Gallop poll studying people from over 200 countries, revealed that 85% of people hated their jobs. Overall, they found that only 15% of workers feel engaged in their jobs and feel a sense of "passion" for and "deep connection" to their work.[2]

I firmly believe we don't need to choose between making good money and doing engaging work. We spend too much of our lives working to not enjoy what we do. I believe we can do work that we're passionate about, while helping others and still being well-compensated so that we can enjoy our lives outside of work.

Ikigai Technique

The Japanese technique known as Ikigai (meaning 'reason for being') consists of four key elements that must come together in order to discover your purpose:

- What you are good at
- What you love
- What the world needs
- What you can be paid for

This is a simple yet effective tool to use in order to evaluate the type of work you wish to do. Putting all of my career paths or 'reasons for being' through the Ikiagi diagram yield positive results for each element.

Writing, Coaching and Transforming Education are all things I love to do and things I believe I am good at (and will get better at with continued learning and practice). I also believe honest expression through writing, empowering lives through coaching and expanding minds through education are what the world needs more of. Lastly, I believe I can provide enough value to the lives of others in order to be compensated for these things.

How Do I Find What I'm Passionate About!?

Yes, I know this is the burning question for most people. I think I'd be lying if I suggested there was one simple technique to help you find the answer. Some people discover their passions through intensive inner-reflection while others do it by the brute force method, trying lots of different jobs until they find one they enjoy. Some passions can be born out of necessity, while others seem to just stumble upon passions by chance.

The most effective way to actively search for passions is through inner-reflection methods and that is what I will be covering in the book. You can also engage in the brute force method of trying many different jobs. The downside here is that there are thousands of jobs out there and it could take you decades to find one you are passionate about. However, if you do some inner-reflection methods first, you will at least have a better idea of what type of jobs you should try.

A study which was undertaken by the Institute for The Future (IFTF) in 2017 along with 20 tech, business and academic experts from around the world, estimated that 85% of the jobs that will exist in 2030 haven't even been invented yet. So even if you apply the brute force method and you are lucky enough to find a job that's right for you, that job will probably no longer exist in ten years time [3].

Before we try to find jobs we're passionate about, we first need to search for missions we're passionate about. While our jobs may change throughout the course of our lives, our missions won't. Our missions will act as the guiding light that helps us choose the type of work we can do to advance towards it.

Let's Define Passion

In order to find what we're passionate about it is important that we understand exactly what passion is. Many misinterpret passion as something they love to do. Passion is more than that. If you look at the Ikigai diagram above, you will notice that passion is the intersect between what you love **and** what you are good at.

Examples

1. Construction

Construction work is something I'm not passionate about. While I've done plenty of construction work in the past, I still struggle to bang a nail in straight on my first go. I neither love it nor am I good at it, therefore, it is missing the two core ingredients that define a passion.

2. Surfing

I love surfing but I wouldn't say I'm passionate about surfing. I love going to the beach, renting a board and getting out in the water. It's fun trying to get up on the board and succeeding on occasion. But I've only gone surfing about five times over the past five years. I haven't done enough consistent practice to actually get good at it. Therefore I might pick up a surfboard when the opportunity arises but until I get good at it, I don't see myself jumping out of bed at 5am in November and driving two hours to Sligo to catch the morning waves.

3. Maths

I've always been good at maths but I don't love maths. I thought that because I was good at it, I should do a maths and statistics-based course in college. While I found maths easy in college, I never grew to love it. Therefore maths doesn't make it onto my list of passions either.

4. Writing

I love writing and I'm good at writing (at least I think so). When I was in primary school I used to enjoy writing essays but I was never the best writer in my class. I was better at maths and business type subjects and that's what I pursued in secondary school and college. It was only years later that I picked up writing again. I wanted to try and express myself and I chose to do this in the form of poetry. I realized I really enjoyed it and after a lot of practice, I started to get quite good. Now writing has turned into one of my main passions.

Finding Your Passion is an Art

Because finding your passions can be more like an art than a science, I've done my best to provide you with the right tools so that you can paint a clearer picture for yourself to see where your own passions may lie.

I decided it was better to provide you with all the tools rather than to try and develop one specific formula that I couldn't be sure would work for everyone.

So without further ado (ado is a weird word when you write it down), let's take a look at the first tool!

CHAPTER 2:
FIND A REASON TO MOVE FORWARD

"Those who have a why to live can bear almost any how" - Friedrich Nietzsche

A Journey to My Why

After over two years of actively searching, I eventually discovered a clear vision of my why. Your why is your reason for doing everything you do. It is what gets you out of bed in the morning to pursue your dreams.

I found my why at the bottom of a mountain in New Brunswick, Canada. In August of 2019, I decided to undertake an 1800km cycle from Montréal, Quebec to St John's, Newfoundland. I didn't even like cycling at the time and despite getting good at it, I still wouldn't put it in the passion category. But I chose to undertake the journey because I wanted to do something that pushed me past my mental, physical and emotional limits. My two years in Canada were coming to an end and I was still uncertain as to what I really wanted for my future. I saw the cycle as a chance to get away from all the distractions and noise around me. I hoped it would give me an opportunity to listen to what my heart truly wanted so that I could begin to get some real clarity on my direction for the future.

Luckily for me, I got just what I asked for and coming up on two weeks into the cycle, I reached my lowest point. After three days of cycling through New Brunswick's unforgiving mountains, I had become physically and emotionally drained. As I approached the bottom of yet another steep climb, rain began to pour and in my exhaustion, I suddenly became overwhelmed with emotion.

Every part of me wanted to quit. Tears streamed down my face and I began to question the whole journey. "Why the hell am I doing this? What am I trying to prove to myself?".

But that's when it hit me. A wave of sadness swiftly followed by a crystal-clear vision for what I really wanted. One part of that vision was my family. I longed to be back home with my brothers and my parents.

18

The only other thing I could see was the woman I still loved. The woman who changed everything for me. The one who saw in me what I always wished to see in myself. The one who gave me the courage to truly live. I imagined her at the top of the mountain waiting for me.

Once I could see her there, the pain became more bearable. My suffering had a purpose. If I wanted to be with her someday I knew I first needed to become the man I believed I could be. This cycle was part of that process. It was a test to see how far I'd come and how far I still needed to go. Giving up was no longer an option. A smile crossed my face and my tears subsided. I made it to the top.

Why Your Why is Important

In his book, *Start With Why*, Simon Sinek discusses the importance for individuals and companies to have one crystal-clear why statement. An individual's why statement should consist of one sentence that describes the reason behind everything they do.

Any decision you wish to make about your career should be first filtered through your why statement. Before making a decision, you should ask yourself, "Will this decision move me closer to my why?"

The Golden Circle

Simon Sinek did a famous Ted Talk in which he outlined the Golden Circle and how it worked. In his talk, he refers to how nearly all companies know *what* they do, some know *how* they do it, but very few know *why* they do it.

Most companies focus on building around what they are doing (i.e. the products or services they are selling). He explains the importance for companies to go back and remember the core why that is driving everything they do. The founders of a company often have a clear why for setting it up, but as the company grows in size, this deeper purpose tends to get lost among the ongoing day-to-day activities.

Simon discusses how companies who start with the "why" build greater relationships of trust with customers. Customers who can see why a company does something can relate much easier with them. He uses Apple as an example of a company with a very strong and clear why for doing what they do. For the purpose of understanding how the Golden Circle applies to individuals however, I'll use myself as an example.

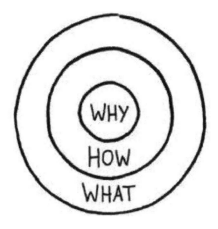

Why (The motivation for everything I do)

To empower others so that they can live lives full of love, joy, and fulfillment.

How (The methods I use to achieve my why)

- Connecting with people on a deep level
- Continually learning and investing in my own knowledge
- Bringing people together
- Leading by example
- Looking for creative solutions

What (The products and services I provide to achieve my why)

- Writing books
- Coaching
- Developing New Models and Courses for Education

In Times of Pain

Not only does your why determine what you do and how you do it, but it also helps to keep you going when you hit the low points. Unless you choose to travel a well-trodden path, going after your dream career is not always going to be easy. There will be moments when you want to give up and you must be able to push past those moments when they arrive. To do that you need to remember and refer back to your why.

When I'm struggling to bring my ideas for education to reality, I think of all the children who might experience unnecessary mental and emotional suffering if I don't succeed. Remembering that my mission is greater than my individual problems, helps me to keep working through any struggle I am experiencing.

How to Find Your Why

You'll be glad to know that there is a method to finding your why. There is a whole book on it in fact. The exercise the book runs you through is based on recounting stories from your past. The stories you will be looking to extract are memories of some of the great highs and extreme lows you have experienced.

In the book *Find Your Why*, Simon Sinek and his team suggest that the Why Discovery exercise is best done in pairs. The purpose of having a partner is so they can help to dig out the main themes from your stories and spot the underlying emotions behind them that may not be obvious to you.

While I agree that it is best done in pairs, I've altered the method in this book so that you can do it by yourself. When I read their book for the first time I did it by myself and I'm guessing you might prefer to do the same at this point. If you have a high-level of self-awareness and you can be honest with yourself, I'm sure the solo approach will work well for you too. Otherwise, I'd suggest finding a partner to help.

Method - Individual Why Discovery

Step 1: Gather Stories

Preparation
In preparation for your Why Discovery process, take out a piece of paper and draw a horizontal line across the page (why not just do it now as your reading?).

Highs
Think back to your past and try to remember times when you felt at your happiest. Try to come up with at least five happy memories. Each time you come up with a memory, draw a dot representing the happy memory above the horizontal line. Rank your happy memories by placing the happiest memories higher above the line.

Lows
Do the same for the times you felt most unhappy. Try to come up with

at least five of your worst memories. Rank them by putting the unhappiest memories further below the line.

Questions to help jog memories for stories

If you are struggling to come up with stories here are some questions to help you:
- Who in your life has helped make you who you are today? Write down a specific time with them. How did they make you feel?
- What is your earliest happy memory?
- What was a great feeling you had at work? What happened?
- What was the worst feeling you had at work? What happened?
- At school, what experience did you love? What experience did you hate?
- What's been a pivotal moment in your life, when things changed forever?
- When did you give up your time to help someone else?
- When have you felt good for doing something that mattered?

Step 2: Record Details and Identify Emotions

For each good and bad memory, write down answers to all of the following questions:
- What specific event was going on when you felt this way?
- Who was there?
- What happened?
- What was said?
- What specific emotions did you experience? Write them all down
- For happy memories was it love, joy, contentment, pride, confidence, satisfaction or something else?
- For unhappy memories was it rejection, sadness, loss, worthlessness, depression, shame or something else?

Step 3: Look for Contributions and Impacts

You want to find the common threads and themes in your stories. The recurring themes will be what your why is based on.

Contributions

How did you contribute in this story? Contributions are what you gave to someone. Positive contributions include things such as lending a listening ear to someone, teaching someone something, showing love to someone, or helping someone. Negative contributions include betraying someone's trust, lying to someone, talking badly about someone, purposely hurting someone.

Impact

What impact did you have in this story? Impacts are the specific effects you had on others. Positive impacts include empowering someone, making someone happy, making someone feel noticed. Negative impacts include making someone feel sad, worthless or unheard.

Step 4: Draft a Why Statement

Your why statement will read as follows:

To *<insert contribution here>* so that *<insert impact here>*

Once you have finished recounting your stories, you should have a list of contributions and impacts you made. Out of these contributions and impacts, there should be one or two that stand out from the rest, representing who you are. Choose one theme for contribution and one theme for impact.

Once you have chosen the themes, take the time to create the first draft of your why statement.

Step 5: Refining the Why Statement

Once you have your draft why statement you can continue to refine it until it sounds right to you. You need to love the words enough to almost want them tattooed on your arm (don't worry, I haven't got mine tattooed yet - I said almost).

One good method to further refine your why statement is to ask your close friends why they are friends with you. They will probably reply with generic qualities that most people expect in a friendship. You must insist that they tell you what specifically it is about you that made them choose to be friends with you. When they start to talk about how you make them feel, that is the answer you are looking for. This will hit you as they are describing the value you have in their life which will often be your why. You can work to incorporate the input from your friends into your why statement.

Tip: If you find this hard to do this face-to-face, try asking them in a text message. It will save you both the awkwardness and it will give your friend time to really think about it before responding.

Alternative Option: Partner Why Discovery

Choosing a partner

It's recommended to do your why discovery process with someone who doesn't know you too well. Close friends or family members may tend to be more subjective when asking you questions due to the beliefs they hold about you already. This may lead them to think they already know what themes to expect instead of keeping an open mind while listening. Some of the stories you want to share may also include close friends or family members and you may not want to hurt their feelings by sharing those particular stories.

If you don't know someone who fits the criteria for an appropriate partner, a good option is to try and source a life-coach. They will be perfectly trained to help you dig into your stories and pull out what's important.

How it works

Step 1: Choose a Time and place

The time it takes for people to complete a Partner Why Discover varies, but it is recommended you set aside three hours. Choose somewhere where you won't be disturbed and due to the intimacy of the conversation, it is best to do it out of public view.

Step 2: Share stories

Now it's time to begin sharing your stories with your partner. Try to focus on recounting specific memories. Try to include details, such as the feelings you experienced and the conversations you had. Out of the then stories you wrote down in preparation, try to detail 5 or 6 stories in full.

Step 3: Identify themes

It is your partner's job to listen intently and objectively to your stories to try to extract the main recurring themes and patterns of behaviour. For each story, your partner should pull out the main feelings you experienced as well as any contribution you made and any impact you had.

Step 4: Draft a Why Statement

This process is the same as in the individual why discovery except you and your partner will both be creating your why statement.

Along with your partner, choose one theme for contribution and one theme for impact out of the lists you have for both.

Once you have chosen the themes, you should both write independent first drafts for five minutes. Share the drafts and choose which one you like best - maybe you can combine them.

Remember the formula is:

To *<insert contribution here>* so that *<insert impact here>*

Step 5: Refining the Why Statement
This is the same as for the individual method

Tips For Your Partner

- Your goal is to have a draft of their why statement at the end
- This is who they are at their natural best
- You must remain unbiased and fully present. This is not a therapy or mentoring session
- Engage in active listening. Hear more than just the words being said. Take note of body language, tone and pauses.
- Make sure to get specific examples
- Dig deeper than the facts, get to the underlying meaning
- Look for person's contribution and impact for each story
- Avoid leading questions
- Avoid why questions (use what instead)
- Be silent and let them struggle for words. When they are struggling it is often because they are processing difficult emotions. It could often lead to an important insight.

Defining My Why

After doing my Individual Why Discovery, the themes I found in my stories were:

- Love
- Joy
- Friendship
- Helping others
- Low Confidence

From my stories, I crafted a **why statement** which now helps guide me in everything I do. My why statement is:

To empower others so that they can live lives full of love, joy, and fulfillment.

That statement fits into why I'm writing this book. It fits with why I choose to coach people. It's why I want to change the education system. I want to empower people. I want to show people how they can become the heroes of their own lives. To show them they can become who they want to be and that they can find love, joy, and fulfillment. If I can, anybody can. For years I suffered from extremely low confidence and I never believed myself worthy of love. It took me a long time to build my confidence and believe I was worthy and now I want to help show others how to get there.

CHAPTER 3:
DETERMINE THE RULES OF YOUR ROAD

"It's not hard to make decisions when you know what your values are" - Roy
Disney

When I started off on my cycle I didn't plan much. I don't like trying to plan things when there are too many unknowns. I had my final destination in mind and on the day I set off, I commanded Google Maps to guide me towards a town that was a reasonable 80km away.

While I believe planning isn't needed in certain areas, one area I should've put more thought into before my departure was the rules of the road I was going to live by. Without rules and ethics to live by, making everyday decisions on the bike became more difficult. What constituted as a successful cycle to St Johns? Was I allowed to stop for a day or two to rest? Did I need to cycle every mile or could I walk very steep parts? Was I allowed to get a lift with a passing car if I broke down? Was there a time limit?

While I contemplated a few of these questions before departing, I never made any strict rules about them. I thought I would just figure it out on the road but this laid back attitude led to a moment of poor decision-making that still disappoints me looking back now.

A Moment of Poor Decision Making

After cycling through the hills of New Brunswick for three days, I arrived at the house I was staying a broken man. I was physically and mentally drained. After a good feed and a good sleep, I awoke to a lovely breakfast to set me up for another day of cycling. As I ate my breakfast and sipped on my coffee I looked out the kitchen window as rain lashed down from the heavens. "I don't fancy cycling in that" I thought to myself .

I began chatting with the other girl who was staying in the house and she told me she was driving to Miramichi after breakfast. "That's where I plan to cycle to today!" I said. "It's about 100km from here right?" She nodded in agreement. "Do you want a lift?" Suddenly my mind descended into an internal battle.

Weak Cormac: "Could I get a lift with her to Miramichi?

Strong Cormac: "No, I can't. I better cycle all of the 1800km. That's what I set out to do."

Weak Cormac: "Yeah but it's pissing rain outside and your legs are wrecked. Plus you have that e-book revision due today and you could do with saving time by driving there"

Weak Cormac disguised as Strong Cormac: "Wait a second, this is my trip. I make the rules. It just makes sense to get a lift, especially when it's laid in front of me like this. It must just be a sign to take it. Plus, I love meeting new people and it will be good to get to chat in the car"

The day before I reached my final destination at Cape Spear lighthouse, I calculated how many kilometers I had covered. I hoped I would have gained some extra kilometers due to the need to go off route to stay in different places along the way. Unfortunately, I hadn't realized that by cycling along a few highways in my last week, I was cutting into my kilometers (I had calculated 1800km using the bicycle trails). When I finally reached Cape Spear after a month on the road, I was just over 100km short of the 1800km I said it would take to get there.

This made reaching Cape Spear somewhat of a hollow victory for me as I felt I had cheated myself. I wanted to cycle an extra 150km the day after finishing to make up for it but by the time I reached Cape Spear, my back tire was ready to fall off at any moment. In the end, I just had to admit that I fell 100km short. That one moment of weakness in week 2 came back to bite me in the end.

Why Your Rules Are Important

The rules of the road are the core values and principles you live by. You must have your values clear in your mind if you wish to live in alignment with the person you wish to become. If you don't have clearly defined values from which you can develop solid principles, moving towards your destination will be filled with lots of difficult decisions and lots of resentment for decisions made at weak moments.

Having said this, try not to be too hard on yourself when you do break your own rules. You will inevitably steer off the road every now and again. The important thing is to have your rules in place so they can keep you on track for the majority of the journey. Initially, I felt very disappointed in myself for my moment of weakness but afterward, I realized that reaching Cape Spear was still a great achievement overall.

Values vs Principles

Values are the qualities and personal characteristics that we believe are most important to us. We often develop our values at a young age by modeling people we look up to. For example, we may have taken values from our parents, siblings, teachers or friends.

Principles are the rules that govern our behaviour. They are developed based on our values in order to keep us in alignment with them. For example, if respect is one of your core values, you may develop a principle to always say thank you to the bus driver as you get off the bus.

Once you have your values and principles predetermined, the need to contemplate long over decisions no longer exists. You simply know the best course of action to take. If I had predetermined a principle that I had to cycle all of the 1800km in order to keep in line with my value of integrity, then I wouldn't have even entertained the option of getting a lift. I would have simply said "Thanks, but I can't".

All of the great leaders throughout history seemed to possess a unique ability to make important decisions when the pressure was on. Their power didn't always come from an increased intellect, however, it often came from their ability to process any situation through their very clear set of values and principles.

"Once I make a decision, I never think about it again." - Michael Jordan

Method - The Eulogy

This method is taken from Stephen Covey's book *The 7 Habits of Highly Effective People*. For this exercise, I would suggest you find a quiet place where you won't be interrupted. I would also suggest you have a pen and piece of paper beside you.

Clear your mind of everything else. Don't worry about your current schedule, your exams, your job, your family, your friends. Just relax and open your mind to what I will suggest you do.

Close your eyes and imagine yourself walking into your local church. As you enter you can hear soft organ music playing and notice flowers distributed around the seats. As you walk along the aisle you see your neighbours and work colleagues. They look sad and dejected. Then as you walk further up the aisle you see your family and close friends. Many of their eyes are filled with tears. You wish to console them but you notice a casket in front of the altar.

You make your way towards it and take a look inside. You jump back in horror when you notice it is you who is in the coffin. This is your funeral, three years from today. Everyone in the crowd has come to pay their respects and say goodbye.

As you take your seat at the front, you look at the program in your hand and see that there are going to be four groups of speakers. One group is your immediate family and extended family - your mother, father, brothers, sisters, as well as your partner and children. The extended family includes speeches from your grandparents, nieces, nephews, uncles, aunties and cousins.

The second speaker is one of your closest friends, somebody who knows how to describe the type of person you were. The third speaker is someone you worked with. The fourth is someone from the local community.

Think about each of these speeches. What would they all have to say? How would they describe the type of person you were? What kind of husband or wife were you? What kind of father or mother were you? What kind of son, daughter or friend were you? What were you like as a working associate or community member?

What character traits would you like them to have seen in you? What kind of life will they say you have lived? What achievements and contributions would you hope they remember? Look closely at all of the people there. How would you have liked to have made a difference in their lives?

Before moving any further, take the time to write down your impressions for each of these people.

Finding Core Values

If you took the time to do the exercise properly, you will have tapped into some of your deep, core values. These are what drive you on a deep level.

- Look at what you've written and pick out all of the values people talked about you having
- Try to get a list of around ten values that are important to you.
- From this list, choose five values that you believe to be most important for you to represent.
- Try to rank these values in order of importance. This will help you when making a difficult decision in the future.

If you're struggling to think of values you want to embody, here's a list of common values you may want to choose from but try to think of your own too:

- Authenticity
- Caring ✓
- Commitment
- Connection
- Cooperation
- Dedication
- Effort
- Freedom
- Forgiveness
- Friendship
- Gratitude
- Honesty ✓
- Hope
- Integrity
- Optimism
- Patience ✓
- Respect
- Sacrifice
- Unity

Caring
Patient
calm
honest
creative
talented
kind
hard working
ethically conscious.

Core Values and Principles In Practice

To show you how core values and principles come into play in everyday situations, I'll detail an example for you.

Two of my core values are *Friendship* and *Dedication*. While I am dedicated to looking after my health, I have no problem ditching the gym to go drinking with my friends. This is because *Friendship* ranks higher on my list of values than *Dedication*.

I don't necessarily write down all of my principles. Skipping the gym to meet my good mates is just something I know I've no problem doing. While I believe it's important to write down your core values and have them clear in your mind, a lot of your principles will develop over time and through experience. My principles are always being tweaked and changed based on the feedback I receive as I journey through life.

CHAPTER 4:
WRITE DOWN YOUR DESTINATION

"A goal is a dream with a deadline" - Napoleon Hill

Let's talk about goals. Another area of my life I've had plenty of struggles with. In the past, I had a tendency to set extremely audacious goals to be achieved within very short timelines. This often led to a lot of stress and beating myself up for not achieving them. As soon as I set my big goal, other things in life always seemed to get in the way. When setting my goals, I often didn't factor in the other areas of my life that I'd still have to contend with on a daily basis. Things such as work and sport, as well as family and social commitments didn't seem to care about whether I had a new goal or not.

I think that's what turns a lot of people off goal-setting. They see aiming for something they don't have as an unnecessary form of hardship and stress.

Look Beyond the Short Term

When I used to set goals, I often tied my sense of self-worth to whether or not I achieved the goal in question. Most of the time, I failed to achieve my goals and it made me start to question if I just wasn't good enough or if I just didn't want it enough.

In reality, I failed because I didn't have a strong enough *why* behind my goals. I didn't have a compelling enough reason to push me to achieve my goals. What I was missing was a longer-term vision to give my short-term goals meaning. Once I had a greater overall vision in place, I would be able to see how the short-term goals were necessary steps to getting there.

I came to this realization after stumbling on an alternative goal-setting method created by Mindvalley Co-Founder, Vishen Lakhiani. It got me to move away from focusing on low-level goals with tight deadlines that acted only as a means to an end. Instead, I began looking towards higher-level, long-term goals with a greater end result in mind.

Think Bigger

The technique Vishen created is called *The Three Most Important Questions*. The difference with this technique compared with many other techniques is that it focuses on end goals rather than means goals.

Traditional goal setting would probably have you set means goals such as:

- Graduate from college
- Land a job in a big company
- Earn a €100,000 salary by 2021

Means Goals vs End Goals

A means goal is something that is a means to an end. Graduating from college is a means to a greater end. To discover whether a goal is a means goal or an end goal, you must keep asking yourself the purpose behind each goal.

I'll use a character named John as an example. Let's presume John is a student in his fourth year of college and he came to me to help him set goals for his future.

Me: Well, John. Tell me one of your goals
John: To graduate from college with a first-class degree
Me: So what?
John: What do you mean "so what"?
Me: For what reason do you want to graduate from college with a first-class degree?
John: So that I can get a good job in a big company.
Me: So what?
John: So that I can get good experience for my career.
Me: So what?
John: So that I can get promoted after a few years and start to earn more money.
Me: So what?
John: So that I can keep working to save more money and buy a house someday.

Me: So what?

John: So that I can have a home for my wife and kids someday.

Me: So what?

John: What the hell is wrong with you? So we can live in a nice, loving home and have a happy life together I suppose.

Me: (Smiling) Well then, that's your end goal!

Method - The Three Most Important Questions

Now that you know the difference between means and end goals, I'll invite you to do the following exercise.

Take an A4 sheet of paper and draw two vertical lines down the page in order to split it into three separate columns. At the top of the first column, put the heading *Experiences*. At the top of the second column put the word *Growth*. At the top of the third column put the word *Contribution*.

Once you have your three columns it is time to start writing down your goals for each area for the next ten years.

Experiences (To Do)

Take out a timer and spend two minutes writing down all of the experiences you wish to have in the next ten years. What memories would you like to have with people? What places would you love to visit? What adventures would you like to have?

Don't worry, there is no limit on the number of things you can write down and you can always come back to this later and add more if you wish.

The purpose of doing it within a two-minute window is to help you shut off the rational part of your brain that will start to overthink each goal. Allow yourself to write freely about what you really want and remember that no goal is out of reach.

Growth (To Be)

In the second column, you will repeat the two-minute exercise but this time you will be including all the ways in which you would like to grow in the next year. What new character traits would you like to embody? What hobbies, sports or languages would you like to learn? What new skills would you like to have? What books would you like to read? What courses would you like to do?

Again write freely and honestly for two minutes and then stop.

Contribution (To Give)

In the final column, you will repeat the two-minute exercise once more. This time you will include all the ways in which you want to give back to others. What problems do you see in the world that you'd like to help eradicate? What contribution would you like to make to your family? What about your community? What way would you like to treat strangers you meet? What ways would you like to use your money or skills to help others?

The Fourth Most Important Question

Look at your three goal lists. In order for you to have all of those experiences, create all of that growth and make all of the contributions you wish to make, what type of *Career* and *Income* would you need to have? Again, take two minutes to write it all down.

Move onto a new page and begin by writing down:
- The different types of work you would need to do to have all of the impact you wish to make with your *Contributions*. How much money would you need to make to help all of the causes in your *Contributions*?
- The different types of work you would need to do to achieve all of your *Growth* goals. How much money would you need to be able to invest in your *Growth*?
- How much money you would need to make each year to enjoy all the *Experiences* you want to have? How many hours per week would you need to work in order to have enough free time to undertake all of these amazing *Experiences*?
- What else do you want from your *Career* and *Income*? What do you want your working environment to look like? Where do you want to work from? How much money do you want to have in investments? What types of investments would you ideally put your money in?

"All men dream: but not equally. Those who dream by night in the dusty recesses of their minds wake up in the day to find it was vanity, but the dreamers of the day are dangerous men, for they may act their dreams with open eyes, to make it possible" – T.E. Lawrence

CHAPTER 5:
LET THE RAS BEGIN

"Make a Choice. Just decide what it's gonna be, who you're gonna be, how you're gonna do it. Just decide. And from that point, the universe will get out of your way" - *Will Smith*

The Reticular Activating System

The reason the action of writing down your goals is so effective is that it engages the Reticular Activating System (RAS). The RAS is the part of your brain that is responsible for deciding what inputs from your environment it should focus on. We are constantly being bombarded with millions of bytes of information every second yet our brains can only process less than 1% of this information. The job of the RAS is to filter out all of the unimportant information so that our brains can take in what opportunities will most likely move us towards our goals.

By writing down your goals and reviewing them regularly, you are literally telling your RAS what destination you wish to go. The RAS acts like Google Maps. All it needs from you is the final destination and it will work in the background to figure out the best route. Even if you take the wrong route initially it will recalculate to get you back on track.

For example, years ago I used the three questions technique and one of my *Experience* goals was to write a book. I set that goal a few years before I even found writing enjoyable. Looking back now, it seems I wrote that goal as writing was a passion that lay deep inside me. And now here I am, writing a book!

I'm not saying the RAS will bring you exactly where you want to go. It's Google Maps, not a self-driving car. It will guide you if you keep your goals close in mind and trust your instincts. You still have to be in the driver's seat and try to avoid any potholes when they appear. And if Google Maps (your instinct) is trying to send you on a new route, trust it. The route you take to get there is irrelevant, it's the destination that is important.

Make a Decision

Ok so if you're still reading this, I hope you've already decided that you do want it all. I hope you've realized you can find a career you're passionate about, make money doing it and have plenty of time to enjoy your life outside of work too.

Making the decision that you want it all is the first and hardest step to take. But you can only move forward once you make the decision. The Latin meaning of the word decision is "to cut off". By deciding you want it all you must cut off all possibilities of settling for something you aren't completely happy with.

Moonshots

Naveen Jain is currently the CEO of three companies - Viome, MoonExpress and Intelius and he has founded many more. Naveen works to set up companies in some of the most difficult and groundbreaking industries. With his company Viome, he is revolutionizing healthcare and his company MoonExpress is competing with SpaceX and Virgin Galactic to provide affordable, commercial flights to the moon.

In his book, *Moonshots*, Naveen talks about how it is almost easier to achieve big, audacious goals (moonshots as he calls them) than it is to create a small business for yourself. By tackling huge problems such as global healthcare and space travel, Naveen finds it easier to draw people to help him with his audacious missions. When he decided to set up his companies, he knew nothing about healthcare or space travel but he thought it could be improved so he decided to give it a shot. Inspired by the boldness of his mission, people with the greatest knowledge in those areas wanted to work for him. Then people with extraordinary amounts of money wanted to invest in the business.

So if you intend on chasing your dream career, make it easier for yourself and think big. And if your dreams happen to benefit the lives of others, I'm sure plenty of people will be willing to join your cause.

Even if you never fully accomplish your moonshot it doesn't matter. By aiming that high you will probably achieve a lot more than most people ever do in their lives.

"Shoot for the moon. Even if you miss you'll land among the stars" - Les Brown

No Thanks, I'm Happy Here On Earth

I'm aware that shooting for the moon isn't for everyone. Many of us just want to enjoy our lives while doing work we have a passion for. We don't all want to try and build spaceships and lead a team of astronauts on a mission into the unknown.

But that's the good part. For every person shooting for the moon there is a team joining them on the mission. So if you don't want to go out and be the ground-breaker, try to join the team of someone else who is pursuing a dream very similar to yours.

This can work well for you in the long term if the dreams of the person or company you are working for are aligned with yours at the core. Before joining another company or mission, however, make sure you are clear on their why and make sure it resonates with yours.

"Alone we can do so little, together we can do so much." --Helen Keller

CHAPTER 6:
ENJOY THE RIDE!

"You don't go to a symphony to hear the last note" – *Alan Watts*

Why It's Important

If you want to get somewhere, you obviously need to know your destination. Once you set off in the right direction, you will see your life as a journey towards that endpoint. The problem a lot of us have with setting goals and far away destinations is that we cannot get immediate pleasure from them. Your vision may be so far away that you may never actually achieve your ultimate goal. Because of this, it is important that we are enjoying the journey to get there. Again this sounds a bit cliche but if you know how to do it properly, it can make a big difference to your experience of life.

Halfway through my cycle, all I wanted to do was finish. I thought once I finish, I'll be fulfilled and I'll feel great. And yes, as I cycled uphill around the last bend and watched Cape Spear lighthouse come into view, I felt a wave of pride that I hadn't known in years. I was euphoric for the evening and I celebrated with a big dinner and a nice glass of whiskey (courtesy of my wonderful HelpExchange hosts). But the next morning, my mind suddenly shifted towards the next task. Where would I go from here?

When moving towards your big goals and dreams, there is a tendency to put all your happiness in the future achievement of the goal or dream. It is important to realize that the purpose of the dream is not to actually reach the final destination. In fact, as soon as you begin to get close to reaching your destination, you should set another greater destination to strive towards. The point of the destination is to get you moving in the right direction towards what you want in life. There is no endpoint that you must get to. The entire reason for the journey is to enjoy who you become in the process. Setting a destination almost out of sight will help you to reach your true potential as a person, enjoy amazing experiences with the people you love and do great things along the way.

Tell People About Your Dream

Start telling people about your dreams for your career. When you say it out loud it makes it more real and the chance that you actually achieve it becomes greater. Obviously, plenty of people will tell you you've lost it but if you can manage to push past caring what others think then you're already halfway there.

"If people aren't calling you crazy, you aren't thinking big enough." - Richard Branson

The other benefit of telling people about your dream is that they may refer you to resources or other opportunities that might help you. Instead of just your RAS working on it, others will be more tuned into it too. I often get messages from friends about writing opportunities or books they think I should read.

You Don't Need to Quit Everything

We all love to fantasize about dropping everything we're doing, jumping off the boat and swimming to the island to where our dream career lies. But that's not often the best option for everyone (unless you're already a really good swimmer). You don't need to jump out of the boat straight away. Instead, you can stay in the boat for now and start paddling each day to redirect your course. I tell my story as if I jumped from IT to writing but it was a much more gradual process of steadily drifting towards writing. Yes, I quit my IT job but I took other jobs to make money while I was still honing my writing skills. I took jobs that would give me the time and money I needed to put my energy into writing. Eventually, I became good enough to know how to swim by myself and I when I finally jumped I was only a few feet from the shore.

It Gets Easier As You Go

"Every day it gets a little easier… But you gotta do it every day — that's the hard part. But it does get easier." - BoJack Horseman

Once you become really passionate about something it will not feel like a struggle anymore. When you get good enough at it and you love it enough, you will no longer need to push yourself to do it. There will be a point where your passion starts to pull you along. Some people say passion is that thing you can't not do. For example, if someone told me I couldn't write anymore, I think I'd go crazy.

Create a Portfolio of Work Instead of One Painting

Don't get stuck with the belief that there is only one thing you are destined to do with your career. Discovering new passions at different periods of your life will lead you to do many different things throughout your career. Once you have your destination clear, you can decide to try all of the weird and wonderful roads to get you there.

Your Dreams May Change Over Time

Don't worry about choosing a dream now and needing to stick to it forever. If you lose interest in something or fall out of love with a particular passion, that's ok. We are constantly growing and evolving as humans and what you value now won't necessarily be the same as what you value in ten years' time. So chase what you desire now and if that changes down the line don't be afraid to change your direction too. Your heart knows what you really want. Learn to listen to it and have the courage to follow it. Come back to revisit and add to your long-term goals when you feel you need to. As I said in the beginning, this is an art, not a science. Trust your gut and don't look back!

There Will Be Plenty of Time to Look Back

Looking back on the cycle, I remember the best moments as well as the bleakest moments. The best moments are the ones I feel most grateful for and the bleak moments are the ones I feel most proud of overcoming.

When you look back on your life, you won't remember all the mundane and mediocre moments. You'll remember the euphoria of your highs and the character you built in the pain of your lows. Chasing your dreams will likely be full of highs and lows. Settling for an average career will be a much more stable and smooth ride. Would I look back on my cycle with as much joy and pride if I didn't experience the rush of speeding down mountains and the pain of climbing up them? Would it have been even worth remembering if the terrain was all flat and smooth?

Choose a Life Without Regret

"Live as if you were living a second time, and as though you had acted wrongly the first time." - Victor Frankl

Many people believe their biggest and most audacious dreams are out of reach. The older they get, the more 'realistic' they become. They look around and realize no one else they know has achieved any of their great dreams either. They convince themselves that they are happy to settle with what they have too. Who are they to ask for more from life?

As the routine of work helps life speed by, their dreams slowly start to wither and die inside them. Maybe at the end, they'll look back and wonder where all the time went. They'll wonder what happened to those great dreams they had when they were young. They'll wonder what the hell they were so afraid of.

I'll end with this uplifting fact about death.

A study done on the most common regrets of the dying showed the number one regret to be:

"I wish I'd had the courage to live a life true to myself, not the life others expected of me."

CHAPTER 7:
MORE TIPS ON FINDING YOUR PASSION

If you've made it this far and you still haven't discovered anything you're passionate about, here are more tips that will hopefully help you as you go about your daily life.

Try Things

"Just do it" - Nike

Your passions won't always find you, it's up to you to go out and find them. Try different things you think you might have an interest in. Try to stick with them until you get relatively good. If you get good at something and you still don't like it then ditch it and try something else. Remember, passion is what you love and what you're good at.

Don't worry about failing at things when you are searching for your passions. Look at it as a process of elimination. For everything you're good at there will be something else you're fairly bad at. So don't worry about trying something and being useless. I did a lot of construction work during my travels but I wouldn't recommend hiring me to do any work on your house.

Trust Your Instincts

"Deep down you already know the truth." - Anonymous

Sometimes the more we try to grasp at something, the further away we get from catching it. Take the time to sit quietly and listen to your instincts. Often your subconscious mind will already know what you truly want, you just have to get your overthinking brain out of the way. This is why we tell you to set your goals in a short timeframe - to distract the conscious mind and let the subconscious mind speak.

Look Out for Certain Moments

In order to figure out what drives you, you also need to become more aware of how you act in certain situations and environments. There are some moments, in particular, you should pay attention to as they often hold a clue to where your passion lies. These moments include:

Crying

Whether it is tears of sadness or joy, take note of when you cry. It is usually because of something that deeply moved you. Your passions can lie in your pain as well as your joy. I recently watched Tony Robbins: I Am Not Your Guru on Netflix and I had to stop halfway through because I kept breaking out in tears. Because helping people change their lives is what I'm passionate about, watching it happen evokes strong emotions in me.

Selflessness

Notice times when you let go of your ego and forget about yourself. This is one of four feelings we experience when we are in a state of flow. Flow is often linked with action and adventure sports but it can also be achieved when doing something you are extremely passionate about.

Timelessness

The second element of flow is timelessness. Notice moments where you lose all concept of time. Time may either move slower or faster but you are usually left wondering what just happened and how you got where you are.

Effortlessness

Notice moments when things become effortless. This is the third characteristic of flow and it often feels like creativity is flowing naturally through you.

Richness

The final characteristic of flow is when you notice your senses are heightened. Your environment, people and things seem to become brighter and more full of life.

A State of Flow

I often get into a flow state while writing. In this state I become completely oblivious to anything that is going on around me, I lose all concept of time, words flow effortlessly from my fingertips and my intuitive sense is heightened.

CONCLUSION

To sum up:

- Everything on your list of goals is your destination

- Your why is the reason you don't turn back

- Your values and principles are the rules of your road

- Your passions are your fuel

- You are the driver.

Once you are clear on all of these, you can begin to work on building a better car to get you there faster...

That will be what I cover in my next book, *Create Your Career.*

P.S. Don't cheap out and build a bicycle

CONCLUSION 2

After coming this far, I think you should be able to come up with your own conclusion. So why don't you write one yourself?

To help you get started, I'll just ask one question.

"What are you going to do now?"

ACKNOWLEDGEMENTS

I'd like to thank *you* first of all for buying this book and taking the time to read it. I hope it gave you some form of clarity on your future. If it didn't, I'd be more than happy to hear your feedback on how you think the book could be improved. You can send your feedback to *hello@cormacnoonan.com* and if you still don't know your destination (basically if the book failed), let me know in the email and I'd be happy to give you a free coaching call to try and help you find it.

I'd like to thank all my friends who have helped me stay on track with my writing, especially at the moments I questioned myself and what I was doing. And a very special thanks to my team of editors who took the time to read over my messy first draft to bring the book to where it is now. I'm not going to name them but you know who you are.

I'd also like to thank everyone who has followed my blog for the last number of years. Your comments help keep me going too.

To check out more from me, feel free to follow me on the blog: **re-tiredat25.com**

Until next time, go n-éirí an bóthar leat!